I0887294

Food for the Soul: The Recipes of Schubert Ogden

Food for the Soul: The Recipes of Schubert Ogden

Recipes reproduced from recipe cards by
Schubert Ogden
Courtesy of the Ogden Family

Design and Photography by
Rebecca Howdeshell

Bridwell Press

Southern Methodist University
Dallas, Texas
2022

Bridwell Press is the professional publishing arm of
Bridwell Library (SMU Libraries and Perkins School of Theology).

SMU Libraries SMU Perkins

Manufactured in the United States of America

DOI: doi.org/10.3998/mpub.12746627
ISBN 978-1-957946-00-9 (open access)
ISBN 978-1-957946-02-3 (paper)

About the Author

Grandpa Schubert serving Sarah M. Ogden, Rollinsville, CO.

The Rev. Schubert Ogden earned broad renown as a United Methodist theologian—writing challenging books and articles, winning top honors and fellowships, and eventually becoming the subject of younger scholars' analyses. But at Perkins School of Theology, Ogden was known for the tough love he showed pastors-in-training and other seminarians. He demanded as much clarity and depth in their papers and classroom debates as they could muster.

"I've had generations of Perkins students tell me, 'He taught me how to think,'" said the Rev. Charles Wood, a former colleague at Perkins. The Rev. Lovett Weems was one of those students in the late 1970s. "'Intimidating' is not too strong a word," Weems said of Ogden. "But I don't mean that in a negative sense. He had high expectations."

Ogden died June 6, 2019 in Louisville, Colorado, near Boulder and Denver. He was 91.

Among those remembering him with gratitude is the Rev. Philip Devenish, one of his Perkins doctoral students in the 1970s. Devenish had been studying at Yale Divinity School when he read a scholarly article by Ogden and decided he'd found his theological mentor. Devenish and his wife, Phoebe, had never lived outside the northeast but moved to Dallas so he could study with Ogden at Perkins, part of Southern Methodist University. His admiration only grew. "You almost can't overestimate his importance, and the significance of his work," said Devenish.

Born in Cincinnati, Ogden would study at Ohio Wesleyan University, Johns Hopkins University and the University of Chicago Divinity School. His doctoral dissertation at the University of Chicago won the school's award for best dissertation in education, sociology or theology and was published by Harper and Brothers as *Christ Without Myth*, in 1961. The book was Ogden's response to the German theologian Rudolf Bultmann, with whom he would have a close association. Ogden also was influenced by Charles Hartshorne, a philosopher he studied with at The University of Chicago. "(Ogden) is most noted among theologians for a kind of blend of the existential theology of Rudolf Bultmann and the neo-classical metaphysics that comes out of Charles Hartshorne," Wood said.

Devenish took his own crack at explaining Ogden's work: "Among his important contributions to Christian theology is the recognition that what is Christian and what is true are independent of each other," he said. "There's a historical judgment about what is accurately Christian and then there is a philosophical judgment about what is true. Something being Christian does not make it true, and something being true does not make it Christian, and Christian theology is responsible for both judgments."

Ogden's other books would include *Faith and Freedom*, *The Point of Christology*, *Doing Theology Today* and *The Understanding of Christian Faith.* Devenish recommends for general audiences two Ogden books of later years – *To Preach the Truth: Selected Sermons and Homilies* and *To Teach the Truth: Selected Courses and Seminars.*

In 1956, Ogden — still working on his doctoral dissertation — joined the Perkins faculty. As his star rose, other seminaries tried to hire him. Ogden did leave in 1969 to become University Professor of Theology at the University of Chicago, but returned to Perkins and SMU in 1972. Two years later, he became director of the Graduate Program in Religious Studies. He retired from Perkins in 1993. Along the way, he won a Guggenheim Fellowship, was elected to the American Academy of Arts and Sciences and served as president of the American Academy of Religion. The book "Witness and Existence," published by The University of Chicago Press, collects scholarly essays written in Ogden's honor.

At Perkins, Ogden team-taught courses with John Deschner, and later with Wood and others. The professors often saw things differently, and Perkins' leaders liked that.

"The idea being, you can't get through the course simply by agreeing with the instructor," Wood said. He added that having Ogden as a colleague was "a great gift," and that Ogden didn't try to win him over, but rather tried to help him perfect his own thinking. "If I showed him something I'd written either pre-publication or after it was out, I would always get a detailed, two-or-three page set of notes," Wood said.

Though a scholar through and through, Ogden in the 1950s was ordained as a deacon and then as an elder in the Ohio Conference. He and his late wife, Joyce, were active at Northaven United Methodist Church in their Dallas years. "Schubert was a church-going person, sang in the choir, and was committed to The United Methodist Church and the local church," Devenish said.

Ogden remained intellectually engaged and writing until very late in life. "Notebooks," a book derived from notebooks he kept over decades as he read and responded to other theologians and philosophers and revised his own thinking, was published just last year. Drew Theological School has digitized and made available Ogden's notebooks. Ogden also is well represented on YouTube, where he's featured in a series of American Scholars of Religion interviews. They reveal the formidable intellect that caused fear and trembling among Perkins students.

"He was fundamentally kind and caring, but he saw his vocation primarily as caring about the way students thought, caring about their theological formation, and he wasn't cutting any corners with that," Wood said. Ogden is survived by sons Andrew and Scott and three grandchildren.

Written by Sam Hodges, this article was originally published as "Theologian Ogden pushed himself and his students" by UM News on June 11, 2019. Reprinted with permission.

Table of Contents

Foreword

The idea of food and theology are not all that inseparable. In fact, if we are to consider biblical references to food there are nearly two hundred mentions of both comestibles and eating in the New Testament alone, while the whole Bible has by some estimates over twelve-hundred references. With this in mind, the consideration is not merely *a reference*, but a *centrality*. Indeed, food is at the core of our existence, something that we cannot continue to live without. It is also something that we understand both in terms of its physical reality *and* its metaphoric and spiritual realities. Grain, bread, cheese, honey, butter, meat, broth—these are all the sustenance of the human being throughout *all* time. Words like *nourish, nutrition,* and *nurse* come from the same Latin roots, each inferring a sense of succor, support, and guidance, which is why *food* as an idea and a reality plays a central role in its portrayal and relationship between the body and spirit.

Schubert Miles Ogden (1928–2019), one of the preeminent theologians of the last fifty years, spent a significant part of his career at Perkins School of Theology—and no doubt equally countless hours in Bridwell. He was not known in professional circles for any particular *theology of food*, per se. Ogden produced an extensive theological and hermeneutical oeuvre in the crucible of Bultmann's negotiation of *mythoi* and Hartshorne's empiricism and process philosophy—perhaps an example of Ogden's own *Christological recipe*—among many other significantly important debates. Outside of the classroom and library, though, Ogden was a formidable *theologian of the kitchen*. We might usually say "artist," and we probably still can! But the fact remains that his talents in cooking were not so much *creatio ex nihilo,* as *creatio ex terra*: the land, the earth, the Creation of the world provided the bounty which he crafted with artistry and taste to make wonderful and delicious meals. Perhaps he is not as famous as the so-called "Cooking Priest" Father Leo Patalinghug, who has gained a significant following for his humor, recipes, and feeding the flocks, but Prof. Ogden will now enter the reputable annals of the culinary theological Fathers—the patristic palate, if we may.

Food for the Soul: The Recipes of Schubert Ogden is among the first new publications from Bridwell's new publishing activities. The library itself has published scores of books, catalogues, and other works since the early 1960s, and moves forward with this publication as a monument to both Shubert Ogden's legacy and the variegated aspects of theology, creation, and the natural world he experienced and lived in. Recipes, like theology, are often taken apart, critiqued, and reformed. They have bits and pieces added to them—a little extra grace, a little less pepper, and an extra spoon of salt or salvation—they both change the flavor of a good dish. I want to thank all those involved in bringing this project to fruition, including those who initiated the first inklings of such an idea, namely Prof. Theodore Walker, Jr. and Alex Vishio of Perkins School of Theology; the family and executors of the Ogden estate, especially Philip Devenish; and Rebecca Howdeshell, who tirelessly and enthusiastically took on this and other projects, and enlivened the work with her artistic vision and focus. We hope that you enjoy this book.

Anthony J. Elia
Director and J.S. Bridwell Foundation Endowed Librarian, Bridwell Library
Associate Dean for Special Collections and Academic Publishing

Introduction

Schubert Ogden was a good cook. He was (and remains) a great Christian theologian—in fact, he has put Christian systematic theology on a new basis: His is the first Christian theology ever—believe it or not!—actually to be clear that "Christian" and "true" do not somehow imply each other.

He does argue that a genuinely Christian theology—that is, one whose meaning accords with how, so far as we can tell, Jesus' first followers understood him—is true. But he argues that this is true not because it is Christian, but simply because it is true—true to the experience of each and every human being, experience that for each and all includes the "pure, unbounded love" of the true God. Nobody had related "true to Jesus" and "true" in this way before. But so much for Schubert Ogden the theologian.

As for Schubert the cook. He was not as great a cook, but he was almost as careful and even fussy about his recipes and preparation as he was scrupulously honest and critical as a thinker.

The recipes are mostly German, the legacy of his German-American family from Cincinnati—except for those from Texas and Colorado, which reflect the Mexican and barbecue influence of the Southwest and the Rockies—via Perkins (SMU) and his and his wife Joyce's mountain cabin in Rollinsville.

You won't lose any weight on these recipes. But they are also pared of any extra fat or additives—just like the theology! So, mix, bake, and grill away to your heart's content. The recipes here are good for your heart and soul.

Philip Devenish
Ph.D. SMU '77

We have preserved the content of Schubert Ogden's recipes as closely to his original text and instructions. This includes the retention of abbreviations such as *t for teaspoon* and *T for Tablespoon.* Recipe temperatures may need a slight variation to accommodate for cooking differences in the Rockies, where Ogden lived. Rollinsville, Colorado is at an elevation of 8,671 feet and there may be variation in cooking outcomes at lower elevations. Most remaining conventions should be clear.

OGDEN'S APFELPFANNKUCHEN

1/2 c sifted flour
2 t sugar
1/4 t salt
4 eggs
1/2 c milk
8 T butter
3 sweet/tart apples, peeled and sliced
raisins

1. Sift flour, sugar, and salt together.
2. Whip eggs until light and frothy, then beat in milk.
3. Turn flour mixture into beaten eggs and milk and, still using beater, whip until you have a smooth batter.
4. Plump as many raisins as you'd like for garnish.
5. Sauté sliced apples lightly in butter until they just begin to soften and take on color. Sprinkle well with a mixture of equal parts granulated sugar and cinnamon and set aside.
6. For each pancake, melt 2 T butter in 10" skillet, and pour in enough batter to cover the bottom. Arrange apple slices over the top of the pancake and scatter as many plumped raisins on it as you prefer. Continue to cook over moderate heat until bottom of pancake is brown and the pancake slides easily when moving the skillet. Then add 2-3 T batter over the top of the pancake, and place under a 350° broiler for 2-3 minutes or until the pancake begins to rise toward the heat.
7. Serve at once—sliding each pancake carefully onto its own dinner plate, sprinkling it lightly with confectioner's sugar—and, especially if your apples aren't all that tart, with a lemon wedge on the side that can be squeezed over the pancake to taste.

Makes 3-4 pancakes

Rollinsville, Colorado
Fall, 2014

~ NOTES ~

OGDEN'S BEST-EVER BLUEBERRY COBBLER

Filling

3 c blueberries
4 T sugar
1/3 c orange juice
1/4 c Triple Sec (or equivalent)
1 1/2 t cornstarch dissolved in orange juice or Triple Sec

Topping

2/3 c flour
1/4 t baking powder
1/4 t salt
8 T margarine or butter
1/2 c sugar
1 egg
1/2 t vanilla extract

1. Toss berries, 4 T sugar, orange juice, Triple Sec, and dissolved corn starch in an ovenproof glass or ceramic baking dish. Set aside to marinate for 3 hours or so. (Alternative [which I follow]: Refrigerate and allow to marinate overnight.)
2. Bake marinated berries (untopped) in preheated 375° oven for 20-25 minutes. (Alternative [which I follow]: Remove the marinated berries to a pan and cook slowly on top of the stove, adding more corn starch as necessary, to desired consistency—The object of this step is to reduce the moisture and thicken the consistency without allowing the berries to become too soft or mushy.)
3. Whisk flour, baking powder, and salt together in a small container. Set aside.
4. Cream margarine (or butter) and 1/2 c sugar with mixer until fluffy and light in color. Beat in whole egg and vanilla until smooth. And then slowly incorporate above dry ingredients into mixture, using low setting on mixer.
5. Place berries in baking dish and top with topping, covering as much of the surface as possible with the batter.
6. Bake in preheated 375° oven for 35-40 minutes until topping is golden brown and berry filling is bubbling.
7. Cool briefly before serving—either as is, with whipped cream, or (as we prefer) vanilla ice cream.

Rollinsville, Colorado
Summer, 2008

~ NOTES ~

OGDEN'S CREAM OF CELERY SOUP

1-2 T butter
4-5 c finely chopped celery (with leaves)
1 medium onion, chopped
2 c chicken stock (=2 c canned chicken broth, or 2 c boiling water+3 bouillon cubes)
4 c milk
1 1/2 T cornstarch
Nutmeg
Potatoes*

1. Melt butter in pressure cooker (or skillet) and sauté celery, onion, and potatoes for about 10-15 minutes, or until vegetables soften.
2. Place sautéed vegetables in pressure cooker with 2 c stock, and cook for 15 minutes at 15 pounds pressure.
3. Purée cooked mixture in blender, return to pot. Dissolve 1 1/2 T cornstarch in 1/2 c milk and add to soup together with the remaining 3 1/2 c of milk. Bring to a boil.
4. Either serve as is or season with a grating of nutmeg (to taste) and serve with chopped parsley as a garnish.

*Original recipe card did not include exact potato amount, but they are described in the recipe.

Westminster, Colorado
30 April 2011

~ NOTES ~

OGDEN'S CREAM OF PORTOBELLO MUSHROOM SOUP*

1 lb Portobello mushrooms
4 c chicken broth or bouillon
1/4 c chopped celery
1/4 c sliced onion
1/4 c diced carrot
2 T butter
3 T flour
2 T sherry or cognac (optional)
2 c milk or cream (or mixture)
1 t salt, or to taste
1/8 t Tabasco

1. Prepare celery, onion, and carrot for cooking.
2. Remove stems from mushrooms and chop roughly. Slice mushroom caps and set aside.
3. Lightly sauté vegetables and mushroom stems in butter to bring out flavor.
4. Combine with 4 c of chicken broth and simmer for 35-40 minutes.
5. Drain vegetables and mushroom stems and reserve stock.
6. Puree vegetables and mushroom stems in blender and return to stock.
7. Bring stock back to a boil, stir in butter and flour, kneaded into a thick paste.
8. Add sliced mushrooms to boiling stock and simmer for 10 minutes.
9. Add sherry or cognac (optional).
10. Heat 2 c of milk or cream and stir into stock.
11. Check salt seasoning and add Tabasco.

*Adapted from James Beard's *American Cookery*: 96 and *The Joy of Cooking*: 39.

~ NOTES ~

OGDEN'S CURRIED TURKEY STACK-UP*

1/2 c chopped onion
1/2 c chopped green pepper
1 clove garlic, pressed or minced
2 T butter or margarine
2 c cooked turkey scraps, or turkey meat cut into bite-sized pieces
1 15 oz. can tomatoes, cut up
2 T dried currants
2 T snipped parsley
1-2 t curry powder
1 t salt
1/2 t freshly ground black pepper
dash of ground mace
2 T cold water
1 T cornstarch
1/2 c sharp/extra-sharp cheddar cheese, roughly grated
Enough 6" or 8" corn tortillas (softened in the microwave for 2 minutes at 1/2 [5] power) as may be required to constitute the stack-up in the casserole employed.

1. Lightly grease a casserole capable of containing the stack-up constituted by the layered 6" or 8" tortillas. Set aside.
2. In a saucepan cook onion, green pepper, and garlic in butter or margarine till tender but not browned. Stir in turkey, undrained tomatoes, currants, parsley, curry powder, salt, pepper, and mace. Cook, stirring occasionally, till heated through, ca. 10 minutes. Blend cold water into cornstarch; stir into turkey mixture. Cook, stirring constantly until mixture is thickened and bubbly.
3. To assemble, place one warmed/softened tortilla in the bottom of the greased casserole.
4. Cover with turkey-tomato sauce and top with grated cheddar cheese. Repeat layering tortillas and sauce / cheese as many more times as are necessary to fill up the casserole, ending with the sauce. Sprinkle with the remainder of the cheese. Bake, uncovered, at 350° until heated through, ca. 15-20 minutes. Serves 4.

*Adapted from a recipe in *Better Homes and Garden Crepes Cook Book*, p. 24.
Broomfield, Colorado
Fall, 2009

~ NOTES ~

OGDEN'S DRESDEN (DRESDENER) STOLLEN*

1 1/2 c raisins
2 c candied fruit
1/2 c rum
2 envelopes (4 1/2 t) dry powdered yeast
1/2 c lukewarm water
1 T granulated sugar (optional)
2 c milk, scalded
1 c granulated sugar
1 t salt
1 1/2 c butter
grated rind of 1/2 orange
grated rind of 1/2 lemon
3 T lemon juice
1/2 t freshly grated nutmeg
1/2 t ground mace
2 c flour
4 eggs, lightly beaten
5-8 c flour
1 t almond extract (or 6-8 slivered blanched bitter almonds)
1 1/2 c chopped blanched almonds
melted butter
granulated sugar
confectioner's sugar (if possible, vanilla flavored)

1. Combine raisins and candied fruit, and soak in rum overnight. Drain and reserve rum.
2. Proof yeast in lukewarm water, using sugar to speed the process if desired.
3. Scald milk; melt butter in milk; add salt and sugar, and stir until dissolved. Then stir in lemon and orange peel and lemon juice, reserved rum, spices, and almond extract (if using it instead of bitter almonds).
4. Cool mixture to lukewarm, add yeast and 2 c flour. Mix well and set in warm, draft-free place to rise up to 30 minutes, until dough blisters. Stir in lightly beaten eggs and gradually mix in 5-8 more cups flour until dough is soft and light and not sticky. It should be smooth enough to be handled.
5. Turn dough onto floured board and knead, gradually working in additional flour, fruit, raisins, and almonds (as well as bitter almonds if using them). Keep kneading dough until it blisters and is smooth and elastic and the fruit and nuts are all well mixed in. Gather into a ball and place in a lightly greased bowl. Cover loosely with damp towel and set in warm draft-free place to rise ca. 1 hour or until doubled in bulk.
6. Punch down dough and cut into three equal pieces. Set them aside to rest 10 minutes. Then roll or hand-flatten each in turn into an oval 3/4" thick. Brush top of each with melted butter and then sprinkle with granulated sugar. Fold each lengthwise, not quite in half, so that the edges are within 1/2 - 1" of meeting; pinch closed. Place loaves on lightly greased cookie sheet, placing aluminum foil between them where they touch. Set in a warm draft-free place to rise until doubled in bulk ca. 1 hour.
7. Preheat oven to 400°. Brush loaves with melted butter. Bake 10 minutes uncovered, then turn heat down to 350° F, and, covering the loaves with aluminum foil, bake another 40 minutes until they are crisp golden brown. Brush the warm loaves again with melted butter and sprinkle generously with confectioner's sugar while still warm. Cool thoroughly before cutting and serving, or storing.

Philip Devenish enjoys Schubert Ogden's stollen

Variations

1. In place of the 2 c candied fruit, you may use 1 c chopped citron and 1 c chopped candied orange peel. In fact, you may use any candied fruits you like–angelica, cherries, and so on. You may also use half (white) raisins and half currants.

2. Saxon (Sächsischer) Stollen is made the same way, except that no nuts or fruit are used other than black and white raisins.

3. For Poppy Seed (Mohn-) Stollen, omit all fruits, using almonds only. When the dough is rolled into flat ovals, brush with melted butter and fill with this filling: 3/4 lb. poppy seeds, ground and simmered in 1 c milk 5 minutes with 1 c white raisins; 3/4 c chopped candied citron, 1/2 c granulated sugar, 1/2 t cinnamon, 1 T rum, and a few drops of rosewater. Mix well until pasty; divide into thirds, and spread on each oval of dough. Fold and bake as above.

*Adapted from Mimi Sheraton, *The German Cookbook*: 450 f.
Broomfield, Colorado
Christmas, 2009; rev. Christmas 2010

OGDEN'S FUNGHI MARINATI

2/3 c olive oil
1/2 c water
juice of 2 lemons
1 bay leaf
2 cloves garlic, pressed or bruised with flat of knife
6 whole peppercorns
1/2 t salt
1 lb small fresh mushrooms, whole or divided, depending on size

1. Combine oil, water, lemon juice, bay leaf, garlic, peppercorns, and salt in a 10-12" enameled or stainless skillet, and bring to a boil over moderate heat. Reduce heat, cover, and simmer for 15 minutes.
2. Drop mushrooms into marinade and simmer on low heat for 5 minutes, uncovered, being careful to turn them over continually so that all sides are in the marinade.
3. Turn off heat, cover the skillet, and allow the mushrooms to cool in their own juices.
4. Store in the refrigerator in a glass jar. (They keep well, for several days, even for a couple of weeks.)
5. Serve by thawing the mushrooms-in-marinade for 30 seconds in the microwave, with good French- or Italian-style bread for dipping.

Comment: The original recipe from which the above has been adapted called for using only small button mushrooms whole. Having done that for many years, only to have increasing difficulty in securing the prescribed size and kind of mushrooms, we have finally learned after a good deal of experimenting that the so-called Baby Bellas (young Portobello mushrooms) are the best ever, and that they work equally well either as whole buttons or cut into as many pieces as we find desirable, to keep something like a uniform size and look.

We've also learned that the liquor created by the marinade-together-with-the-mushroom-juices makes the best dipping oil ever.

Rollinsville, Colorado
27 July 2009

~ NOTES ~

OGDEN'S MORNING GLORIOUS MUFFINS*

2 c flour
1 c sugar (equal parts of brown and white)
1 t baking soda
1 t baking powder
2 t cinnamon
1/4 t salt
1 1/2 c grated carrots
1 1/2 c grated apples (tart is good!)
1/2 c grated coconut (sweetened)
1/2 c chopped dates
1/2 c chopped pecans
3 eggs (or 1 egg + 1/2 c egg substitute)
1 c vegetable oil
1/2 t. vanilla

1. Combine flour, sugar, soda, baking powder, cinnamon, and salt in a large mixing bowl.
2. In another bowl combine grated carrots, apples, dates, coconut, and pecans. Combining eggs (lightly beaten), oil, and vanilla, stir into carrots, etc.; and then add to dry ingredients, stirring all together until just moistened.
3. Spoon batter into lightly greased muffin tins (or, as I do, use paper liners), and bake in preheated 375° F oven for 18-20 minutes.

   Makes ca. 16 large muffins.

*From *Stirring Performance,* by the Comidas Staff at Plaza Resolana, Santa Fe, NM.
All for now. Much love from us both to all of you.
Schubert.

Recipe contributed by Andrew D. Scrimgeour, Ph.D.
Archivist Emeritus, Society of Biblical Literature
Dean of Libraries Emeritus, Drew University

~ NOTES ~

OGDEN'S PFEFFERNÜSSE*

Adam Camas Ogden, cookies with Grandpa Schubert, Westminster, CO December 15, 2018

4 eggs
3/4 c dark brown sugar
3/4 c white granulated sugar
Grated rind of 1/2 lemon
Grated rind of 1/2 orange
1 T citron, finely chopped
1 T candied orange peel, finely chopped
1/4 c grated unblanched almonds
1 t ground cinnamon
1/2 t ground cloves
1/2 t ground allspice
1/2 t ground cardamom
1/4 – 1/2 t ground black pepper
Generous pinch of baking soda
3 heaping c flour
Rum and confectioner's sugar

1. Beat eggs 15 minutes in electric mixer, gradually adding brown and white sugar together. Mixture should be very thick and pale in color.
2. Add lemon and orange rind, citron and candied orange peel, almonds and spices, and mix well.
3. Sift flour together with baking soda and mix into egg-sugar batter.
4. Knead dough on floured board or pastry cloth until smooth. Shape into long rolls about 1 inch in diameter; cut into 1/2" – 3/4" slices; roll into balls in a lightly floured hand; and press flat into circles on lightly greased pan. Allow to dry uncovered overnight at room temperature.
5. Preheat oven to 300°. Turn cookies over just before baking, so that the previously protected soft side will be up. Bake for 20 minutes or until they test done.
6. Brush each cookie with rum and roll in confectioner's sugar while it is still warm. Sprinkle with confectioner's sugar again before serving.
7. Pfeffernüsse keep almost forever if stored in a dry, tightly covered container.

*Adapted from Mimi Sheraton, *The German Cookbook*: 466 f.

Broomfield, Colorado
Christmas, 2009

~ NOTES ~

OGDEN'S PUMPKIN CUSTARD

1 1/3 c Half & Half
1 c dark brown sugar, firmly packed
4 eggs (2 real + 2 funny—or any other combination you prefer)
1/3 t nutmeg
2/3 t mace
1/3 t cinnamon
1/3 t ground ginger
1/3 t salt
1/3 c dry red wine
1 can = 2 c canned pumpkin
whipped cream
rum

1. Scald cream; add brown sugar until dissolved; reserve.
2. Beat eggs well; add all spices and seasonings; beat in pumpkin.
3. Add scalded cream and sugar mixture in slow stream, stirring constantly.
4. Bake at 350° F in well-buttered soufflé dish set in a larger baking dish or pan filled with boiling water up 1/2 " on dish for one-and-a-half hours or until set. Test by inserting table knife all the way to the bottom.
5. Serve with rum-flavored whipped cream.

N.B.: You can simply omit all alcohol without affecting the recipe.

* * * * * * *

The recipe above, which makes 7 servings, is 2/3 of the following, which makes 10 servings:

2 c Half & Half
1 1/4 c dark brown sugar, firmly packed
6 eggs (3 real + 3 funny)
1/2 t nutmeg
1 t mace
1/2 t cinnamon
1/2 t ground ginger
1/2 t salt
1/2 c dry red wine
2 cans = 4 c canned pumpkin
whipped cream
rum

Rollinsville, Colorado
17 September 2013

~ NOTES ~

OGDEN'S RED CABBAGE, OR BLUE KRAUT (ROTKOHL ODER BLAUKRAUT)*

1 2-3 lb head red cabbage
2-3 T butter, lard, or minced bacon
1 T brown sugar
1 large apple, peeled, cored, and chopped
1 medium onion, minced
2 bay leaves
4 T white wine or wine vinegar
1-2 chicken bouillon, as needed
Salt to taste
1/4 c red currant jelly, or preserved *Preiselbeeren*
Flour, as needed

1. Remove all ragged or spotted leaves from cabbage. Cut in quarters, wash, and drain. Shred on cutting board, discarding core and tough ribs.
2. Heat butter, lard, or minced bacon in enameled Dutch oven or casserole. If using bacon, let it melt but do not brown. Add sugar to hot fat and sauté slowly until golden brown. Add chopped apple, minced onion, and shredded cabbage, tossing until coated with melted fat. Add bay leaves.
3. Pour vinegar over cabbage and stir to mix thoroughly. Cover Dutch oven or casserole and braise slowly about 10 minutes, or until cabbage has turned "blue" (= bright purple). Add bouillon, cover, and simmer slowly 11/2-2 hours, or until cabbage is tender. Add more liquid if needed as cabbage cooks.
4. Thicken sauce by adding flour as needed to hot (but not boiling) sauce. Simmer 3-4 minutes until thickened. Season with salt to taste and melt in red currant jelly or *Preiselbeeren.*

*Adapted from a recipe in Mimi Sheraton, *The German Cookbook:* 274

Broomfield, Colorado
January, 2010

~ NOTES ~

OGDEN'S SPRINGERLE*

4 large (or 5 medium) eggs at room temperature
2 c granulated sugar
1/2 t anise oil (not extract), or 2 T crushed anise seed
3 1/2-4 c all-purpose flour
1 t baking powder
1/4 t salt
1 t vanilla extract

1. Beat eggs with electric mixer 15 minutes, gradually adding sugar while beating. Beat 5 minutes more and add anise oil and vanilla extract. Then beat 1 additional minute. (Crushed anise seeds may also be added in the same way. And one may use *both* anise oil *and* some crushed anise seeds, to taste.)
2. Meanwhile, sift together flour, baking powder, and salt several times. Stir ca. 2/3 c of the flour mixture into the beaten egg mixture and mix well. Spread most of the rest of the flour on a pastry cloth, and then place part of the dough on the cloth and roll out with a rolling pin to a 3/16" thickness. Gradually work flour on the cloth into the dough, using only as much as is necessary.
3. Lightly flour Springerle mold between each impression. Impress the dough, and cut apart the individual cookies. Place on an ungreased cookie sheet to dry overnight before baking.
4. The next morning bake cookies at 300° F for 18-20 minutes, taking care that the tops do not brown. Trim cookies with a sharp knife while still warm, and then allow to cool 1 hour before storing immediately in a dry covered container.

Makes ca. 48 cookies.

*Adapted 1 December 1986 from Dad Schwettman's Springerle recipe of 2 January 1968. The ingredients are all exactly the same as his; and most of the directions follow his quite closely. (The biggest difference is that, beginning in December 1981, I bake the cookies at 300° F instead of 325° F and deliberately do not brown their tops.)

Broomfield, Colorado
Christmas, 2009

~ NOTES ~

OGDEN'S SOURDOUGH APPLE CAKES

4-5 small tart (preferably Jonathan) apples, peeled, cored, sliced, & cooked in 4 c water + 1/2 c sugar
1/2 c brown sugar
1/8-1/4 t mace
1/2 t freshly ground nutmeg
1 t cinnamon
1/4 c butter or margarine
1/3 c raisins, plumped in warm water
1 recipe of dry baking mix (see below)
1 1/2 c sourdough starter

Dry baking Mix

2 c all-purpose flour
1 T sugar
1 T baking powder
1/4 t salt
1/3 c butter or margarine

1. Mix first four ingredients and, using a pastry blender, cut in butter or margarine until mixture resembles cornmeal.
2. Add 1/4 c sugar and stir through mixture gently with a fork.
3. Drain cooked apples thoroughly and set aside, reserving at least 2 c juice (augmenting it, if needed, with cider or apple juice). Also, drain plumped raisins.
4. In a very large skillet, bring 2 c apple juice, cinnamon, nutmeg, mace, brown sugar, and butter to boil, and cook slowly for ca. 5 minutes to reduce.
5. Add sourdough starter to dry baking mix to moisten thoroughly (adding more starter if needed). Roll out dough (carefully!) into a rectangle 18" x 12."
6. Spread apples and raisins evenly over the dough, and carefully roll up to make an 18" roll. Cut into 12 one and 1/2" pieces and arrange in skillet in the reduced sauce. (A cup or so of the sauce may be drawn from the skillet in advance to pour over the cakes before baking.) Be careful not to put apples within 2" of either top or bottom of the dough, so that it can be rolled up and sealed without breaking.
7. Bake in a 375° oven for ca. 40 minutes. Allow to cool for 5-10 minutes before serving hot, and consider using bowls so as to accommodate a tablespoon or more of light cream or half-and-half.

Makes 12 cakes.

Rollinsville, Colorado
27 July 2009

~ NOTES ~

OGDEN'S SOURDOUGH-BUTTERMILK BISCUITS

2 c all-purpose flour
1/2 t salt
1/2 t baking soda
1 t baking powder
1/2 c (= 1/4 lb) butter or margarine
1/2 c buttermilk (or plain yogurt)
1 c sourdough starter
Optional additional melted butter or margarine

1. Sift together flour, salt, baking soda, and baking powder. Using a pastry blender, cut in butter or margarine until mixture resembles cornmeal.
2. Mix together starter and buttermilk. And with a fork, stir mixture into mixed dry ingredients until a soft dough is formed that clears the sides of the bowl.
3. Turn out on a floured board and knead gently for 30 secs-1 minute. Roll out evenly to 1/4 - 1/2" thickness, and cut into biscuits ca. 2" in diameter. Place on a lightly greased sheet (or pan) with sides touching. Cover and allow to rest for 30 minutes before baking.
4. Brush tops with melted butter or margarine (optional), and bake at 425° for 12 minutes or until tops are golden brown.

Makes 12-16 biscuits.

Rollinsville, Colorado
27 July 2009

~ NOTES ~

OGDEN'S SPINACH RICOTTA PIE

One-crust pie dough

1 1/4 c flour
2 t sugar
1/2 t baking powder
Freshly grated nutmeg to taste (optional)
2 - 6 T ice water
Rounded 1/2 c vegetable shortening

1. Mix flour, sugar, and baking powder – and nutmeg if you're using it.
2. Cut in vegetable shortening until flour mixture resembles cornmeal.
3. Add ice water 2 T at a time until dough adheres into a ball.
4. Roll out dough with a minimum of handling, put it in a glass pie dish, and crimp edges.
5. Prick dough and glaze it with egg white (or yolkless egg mix).
6. Keep refrigerated until filled.

Ricotta spinach pie filling

1 lb fresh spinach, preferably, or 1 10 oz package of frozen spinach
1 lb (or 15 oz package) part skim ricotta cheese
2/3 c crumbled gorgonzola cheese
1 large egg
1/2 t freshly grated nutmeg
1/3 c to 1/2 c flour
8 t grated Parmesan or Romano cheese
8 oz mushrooms, sliced thin and lightly sautéed in butter

1. Thoroughly squeeze moisture from cooked spinach and chop finely.
2. Add ricotta and gorgonzola cheeses, and mix well.
3. Add unbeaten egg, nutmeg, and 4 T of the parmesan or Romano cheese, together with enough of the flour to thicken the mixture without making it stiff.
4. Stir in the mushrooms.
5. Fill the prepared pie dough with the mixture and sprinkle the top with bread crumbs and the remaining 4 T of the parmesan or Romano cheese.
6. Dot with butter.
7. Bake in a 350° F oven about 40 minutes or until lightly browned.
8. Serve hot or cold.

Rollinsville, Colorado
Fall 2006

~ NOTES ~

OGDEN'S S.O.B. BRISKET*

Sarah M. Ogden with Grandpa - Schubert, Rollinsville, CO, 1991

4-6 lb brisket of beef, whole and well-trimmed
1 1/2-2 large onions, roughly chopped
1 clove garlic, pressed (or minced)
2 oz (1/2 of 4 oz bottle) liquid smoke
Salt, garlic salt (or powder), celery salt (or seed) finely ground, to taste
Worcestershire sauce

1. Drizzle liquid smoke all over one side of the brisket and liberally season with salt, garlic salt (or powder), and celery salt or seed).
2. Cover the entire side with chopped onion and 1/2 of the garlic.
3. Quickly turn over in the roasting pan, so as not to lose any more of the onion and garlic than necessary.
4. Repeat the preceding three steps on the other side of the brisket. Cover roasting pan and refrigerate overnight.
5. Six-and-a-half hours before the brisket is to be cut for serving, douse it with Worcestershire sauce.
6. Cover the roasting pan and roast in a 275° oven for 5-6 hours, or until a fork inserted at the thickest point goes in easily. Check occasionally during the roasting to see that there is sufficient moisture to avoid sticking and to provide natural gravy for serving.

Option: After roasting for 5 hours, pour barbecue sauce over the top of the brisket as desired and roast an additional hour.

*Adapted from *Cowboy Cooking*: 128.

Rollinsville, Colorado
Fall 2006

~ NOTES ~

OGDEN'S TO DIE FOR (TURKEY) GUMBO*

Adam and Sarah Ogden, cooking with Grandpa Schubert, Dallas, TX, 1988

1/2 t salt
3 bay leaves
1/2 t ground black pepper
1/2 t ground red pepper
1/2 t ground white pepper
1/2 t thyme leaves, ground
1/2 t oregano, ground
1 c onions, coarsely chopped
1 c green pepper, coarsely chopped or diced
1 c celery, diced
10 oz package frozen okra
1 lb Hillshire Beef Smoked Sausage, cut into 1/8" slices
1 can (14.5 oz) chicken broth
3 1/2 c chicken bouillon
7 T vegetable oil
1/2 c flour
2-3 c cooked turkey scraps, or turkey meat cut into bite-sized pieces
Lea & Perrins Worcestershire and Tabasco sauce to taste

a. Combine salt, black, red, and white peppers, thyme, and oregano. Set aside.
b. Combine chopped onion, bell pepper, and celery. Set aside.
c. In a medium stock pot on medium heat bring chicken broth and bouillon to a low boil and add bay leaves.
d. Meanwhile, using a cast iron skillet, heat vegetable oil on medium high heat for 4-5 minutes, or to smoking point. Add flour a little at a time, stirring with a whisk continuously to make a roux hazelnut in color; add green peppers, celery, and onions, cook 2-3 minutes. Remove roux/vegetables from the heat, add seasonings, and stir until skillet has cooled. Using whisk, or slotted spoon, add roux/vegetables to stock pot until roux dissolves. Add okra.
e. Then add sausage and turkey. Cook ca. 30 minutes on medium heat. Season to taste with Lea & Perrins Worcestershire and Tabasco sauce. Serve on rice. Serves 4-6

*Adapted from a recipe published by Angela Robinson, owner and chef of Ma Me's Restaurant, in a post-Thanksgiving article in *The Denver Post*, December 2002

Broomfield, Colorado
Fall 2009

~ NOTES ~

OGDEN'S TURKEY SAUSAGE*

Old-Fashioned Breakfast Sausage

1 lb ground turkey
1/2 t salt
1/2 t freshly ground black pepper
1/4 t cayenne pepper (or to taste)
1/2 t freshly ground nutmeg
1-1 1/2 t leaf sage, finely crumbled

Mix all ingredients together thoroughly. And use in any way you would use traditional (pork) breakfast sausage. (We commonly shape the sausage into patties for frying and then freeze it —or such of it as we're not using immediately. It freezes well.)

* * * * * * *

Italian Sausage

1 lb ground turkey
1/2 t salt
1/2 freshly ground black pepper
1/4 t cayenne pepper (or to taste)
1/2 t garlic powder (*N.B.*: If you're planning to use the sausage immediately, you may substitute a clove of fresh garlic, pressed and well-mixed throughout the sausage, for a somewhat stronger flavor.)
1-1 1/2 t freshly ground fennel seed

Mix all ingredients together thoroughly. And use in any way you would use traditional (pork) Italian sausage. (We commonly divide the sausage into two equal parts and freeze it. When we're ready to use it, we thaw it and shape it accordingly, e.g., into larger balls for spaghetti or smaller balls for pizza, or roughly crumble it for calzone. It freezes well.)

*Adapted from family recipes for traditional (pork) sausage.

Broomfield, Colorado
Spring, 2010

~ NOTES ~

SCHUBERT'S OWN SALMON LOAF*

2 c flaked salmon, either cold poached or grilled (or 1 14.5 oz can)
2 c cooked rice (i.e. 1/2 c rice, 1 1/3 c water, 1/4 t. oil; mix altogether, bring to a boil, cover, turn to low, and cook exactly 14 minutes)
1/2 c milk
3 eggs, beaten
1 1/2 T minced parsley
1 T melted butter
1/2 t salt
1 T lemon juice
1 1/2 T minced fresh dill
Freshly ground pepper to taste
1/2-1 t hot sauce (i.e. cayenne's hotter sauce)

1. Combine all ingredients, mix well, and spoon into well-buttered casserole or bread pan.
2. Bake at 375° F for ca. 40-45 minutes.
3. Unmold, slice, and serve with mustard sauce.

Mustard Sauce

1 T butter
1 T flour
Salt and freshly ground pepper to taste
1 c liquid (e.g. chicken bouillon)
1 T Dijon mustard

1. Melt the butter in a sauce pan, add flour, stir constantly and cook over medium – low heat ca. 2-3 minutes.
2. Stir in liquid and continue stirring – cooking for several minutes, stirring frequently until mixture thickens. Let simmer for a few minutes, stirring frequently.
3. Add Dijon mustard, stir in well and simmer 2-3 minutes.

   (You may wish to double the recipe for the size of the salmon loaf, in which event, use only 1 1/2 T mustard).

**James Beard American Cooking*: 14-2, 457 f.
Recipe contributed by Andrew D. Scrimgeour, Ph.D.
Archivist Emeritus, Society of Biblical Literature
Dean of Libraries Emeritus, Drew University

~ NOTES ~

Among the stated purposes of the Bicentennial Theological Consultation is "to explore the affinities between the Methodist heritage and some of the most creative trends in contemporary theology and ethics." The assumption of this paper is that at least one of the things that could be reasonably called "process theology" sufficiently qualifies as just such a creative trend to justify exploring the affinities between it and the distinctively Wesleyan tradition of Christian witness. Before we proceed with this exploration, however, it is important to be clear about some basic presuppositions. In assuming, as I do, that the process theology of which I shall be speaking is among the creative trends in contemporary theology and ethics, I naturally presuppose a certain understanding of Christian theology. According to the familiar analysis of "theology" as logos about theos, or thought and speech about God, Christian theology might be supposed to include all such thought and speech about God as is appropriate to the Christian witness of faith. But while there is certainly precedent for this very broad understanding of "Christian theology," it has long since come to be used more strictly to refer, not to all Christian thought and speech about God, but only to such as are involved in critically reflecting on Christian thinking and speaking more generally. Recognizing this, I myself use the term "Christian witness" to designate all Christian thought and speech about God (as well as the rest of Christian praxis) simply as such, thereby reserving "Christian theology" to be used in this stricter sense. Accordingly, I define the proper meaning of the second term as either the process or the product of critical reflection on the validity - claims expressed or implied by Christian witness. Any act of Christian witness, just like any other act of human praxis, necessarily implies, even if it may not express, certain claims to validity—e.g., to the meaningful ness of what is said, to the sincerity of the speaker in saying it, to the truth of his or her assertions, or to the rightness of the norms regulative of his or her actions (Habermas: 174-179).

Minister Margarita

1. Make some fresh lime juice
2. Wet the edge of a glass with the juiced lime
3. Coat the edge of the glass with coarse kosher salt
4. 1 oz triple sec (Mr. Boston)
5. ½ oz lime juice
6. 3 oz tequila (Jose Cuervo Especial)
7. Add ice
8. Stir
9. Garnish with lime
10. Enjoy!

Watch Schubert Ogden Make Live Here!

Moreover, every act of Christian witness expresses or implies a distinctive claim to validity—namely, the twofold claim to be at once appropriate to what is normatively Christian and credible in terms of common human experience and reason. But this claim is obviously problematic in its one aspect as well as in the other, sharp differences between Christians themselves rendering the appropriateness of their respective witnesses clearly questionable, and the even sharper differences between Christians and other interpreters of human existence serving only to cast doubt on the credibility of any of their conflicting interpretations. Thus, by its very nature, the primary level of praxis of which Christian witness is a part creates the need for the secondary level of reflection that is Christian theology. For it is only by the process of critically reflecting on witness in the way that theology has the task of doing that the problematic claim to validity that witness expresses or implies can ever be validated. Given this understanding of Christian theology, the assumption that process theology is one of the creative trends in contemporary theology and ethics implies at least this: process theology is one way of critically reflecting on Christian witness so as to validate its claim to be both appropriate and credible. I stress that the only process theology I myself have ever had any interest in doing is simply a certain way of doing Christian theology in this full sense of the word. While I should not question that some so-called process theologies are quite properly taken to be either only or primarily philosophical—either because they are not Christian theologies at all, being instead a new form of natural theology, or else because their main contributions are to the philosophical rather than the historical or exegetical tasks of Christian theology—still "process theology" in the only sense that I am willing to accept as proper refers to a certain kind of Christian theology, and hence to critical reflection on the appropriateness as well as the credibility of Christian witness.[1]

[1] Schubert Ogden's Minister Margarita recipe surrounded by excerpt from Ogden's "Process Theology and the Wesleyan Witness" in *Perkins Journal*, 37 no 3 (pp. 18-33) Spring 1984. In the manner of Maimonides' *Mishneh Torah*, central text and commentary. Both are significant *texts for the ages!*